Searching For Spectacular

Beautiful in a Dramatic and Eye-catching Way

Ryan Ashley W.

Searching For Spectacular

Beautiful in a Dramatic and Eye-catching Way

Acknowledgements

First and foremost, I give glory to and acknowledge my Heavenly Father Jehovah. This is the most important relationship in my life and propels my thoughts, my goals, and any motivation I can ever have in helping people to better themselves.

Thank you to my family both near and far, and to my friends. I have been shaped through many relationships. Although there has often been distance for several reasons, I am grateful and will never deny any good that has come from you to me. Thank you to my husband and sons for teaching me and providing me with the utmost growth, endurance, and love.

To my audience, clients, and customers that look to me for encouragement and motivation, that value and appreciate any of my work, and reciprocate by also showing me support, thank you so very much. I hope to continue to uplift and be a bright light during these trying and uncertain times.

Chapters and Summaries

The dangers of self-pity

Don't let your eyes make all the choices. Spectacular can be found with other senses. There is a relationship between the eyes, mind, and heart.

It is shrewd to see the calamity and conceal. Use our imagination…make wise choices. Don't be afraid of "no" to you or from you.

Be an individual, don't adopt others journey.

Don't forget your process, even the bad stuff.

Give yourself power by forgiving and moving on.

"Here is where your light starts shining brighter than ever before."

-Ryan Ashley W.

PREFACE

This is the book we've always wanted. This is the book to remind us that:

We are **Capable**.
We can **Do** It.
We **Will** find Spectacular...

...as long as we remember the simple things along the way.

This book has a few simple key reminders that are very necessary for each of us to keep in mind as we travel our life journey. It's an easy read that focuses on the easy concepts that yet for some reason, are sometimes the hardest to apply.

This book is meant to provide gentle nudges and reminders, and to cheer you on in your journey to spectacular, however long it may be.

INTRODUCTION

If you are reading this as some coming of age inspiration, this may not be the read for you… Many writers, novelists, memoirists, whatever you want to call them feel like they have done it. They have found it, they have grown beyond immaturity and vulnerability, they've catapulted themselves into some sort of forevermore satisfaction that the rest of us can only imagine. Now, this isn't to say that growth and change doesn't happen for the better. It most certainly does. Many of my experiences, however, would leave me wanting more every time.

I used to think I was greedy. I used to think that I wasn't being content. I used to think that I wasn't appreciating my circumstances. The "people with the answers" would like to make us feel that way. They'd like to make us feel like if we are questioning, if we are dreaming, if we are still learning, (especially still learning ourselves), then we are less, then we haven't made it or accomplished it (whatever "it" is). If we are not consistent in our career, in our associates, in our friends, in our style, in our thoughts, in our prayers, then we do not have "it together."

What though I ask is "it?" How, I ask, do they know if "it" is "together." These are the concepts that I just have a tough time adopting and believe me I have tried. I have studied, I have reasoned, I have consulted with a higher source, a Godly source. How do I get "it together"? I've asked. Why do I often end up changing things up? What makes me think I am worthy of such variety in my life? How can I be content with my day-to-day happenings? Why am I always searching for spectacular?

From as far back as I can remember I have been a dreamer. My imagination is vivid. I can't tell you how many times throughout my day I indulge in what someone dear to me calls 'Stare Time'. I daydream. I'm not embarrassed to admit it. I daydream often. Why? Am I a bad listener? Am I bored? Do I just have poor focus?

After years of uncertainty, I began to realize that this is part of how I process information. This is part of what makes me who I am. This is part of how I function. This is my way of processing and playing out my life, my next move, or even what I'm being told.

It's important for people to understand how we function day to day so that we understand why we've personally come to conclusions within a particular scenario or made certain decisions in our lives. Our unique process leads us to our personal choices and results. When you think of it, when we consider our personal make up, are we ever able to truly recreate someone else's story exactly how they experienced it and thus recreate their success? Why not? Most appropriately, they are different than us. How many people can truly tell you all the steps they have taken to get where they are at a certain point in their lives? Some try to explain it. Some try to create a map for you, a self-help series of events that they feel are the highlights of their specific story. "You can do it too", they say.

Likely though, when a successful (what most view as successful) story is dissected, that life changing moment, you know the kind people mention where this happened, that happened, and boom "Success". Likely, these moments are not always planned, are not always expected, and are not always controlled. Some of the biggest things that make each person's road to success different are often the things that go unnoticed along the way.

The things we like and gravitate towards, create the differences in our unique story. I understand goals. I understand having a goal and setting up our circumstances to achieve that goal. I understand the concept of following a model meant to be replicated. Yet, how many of us have followed the model and still not achieved our goal? Why? Are some people just more fortunate than others?

Simply put, the moment is not ours. So, what does this mean? What do we do? My suggestion? Keep searching for spectacular. Not achieving a goal, not appearing to have it together does not mean failure. It simply means we get to keep going. Keep dreaming. Keep praying. Your moment will come. Your spectacular moment when the rhythm flows productively between the things you gravitate towards and the decisions you make because of those things, will come. In the meantime, it's important to know who we are and to do what we like and to know that if those things happen to mutate and change along the course of our life journey, it is okay.

No matter how quirky, how unique, how awkward we may feel, we are never alone really. There is one thing that many of us have in common. We want spectacular. We are all on this journey called life and we move towards the bright and shiny. We gravitate towards the things that catch our eye. It's different for each individual but we all have something, things, or persons that directly influence our choices. Again, these things directing our lives and choices are not always planned, are not always expected, and are not always controlled. These are the functions, the habits, of our inner selves that have grouped us together with other souls at different periods in our lives.

Let's look at where our circumstances are in this very moment for example. Where are we? Who is with us? Who is not? No matter the circumstances of our life, there was a life course filled with choices thus far that landed us where we are in this very moment. You landed you here. Good or bad.

So, what is the point?   The point is that it's not necessarily a specific goal that gets us where we are going, it's us. So, if we are not satisfied with where we are at, we must change ourselves. I'm speaking in general terms here. Of course, I'm very much aware that things happen that are completely out of the scope of human control. Also, I'm not contradicting the thought that it's important to be our unique selves. I'm talking about taking moments in our life to have a periodic examination of ourselves, our circumstances, and our surroundings and ask ourselves if we are okay with these things. If so, great, perhaps your moment of rhythm and balance, your moment of spectacular has come, and you have held on to that moment for a time. It's working for you. But what if when we look, when we make this inventory of our lives, we do not like what we see? Change the necessary things.

What are the things that need changing?   Is it a Personality flaw? Is it something as simple as dietary intake, or how much television viewing we are allowing ourselves to do, something habitual? Is it a much bigger change that is needed such as in career, education, association, or even spirituality? Here's the caveat, the warning.   When analyzing aspects of our lives, it is important to protect our uniqueness. Keep who we are but change our desires. Only change our view of bright and shiny because ultimately, that's why we are where we are. Also, only change it if it needs to be changed.

You see, those views, what we like, what we gravitate towards are what shape our individual journey. These are the ideas that cause everyone's moment to be different despite walking similar paths. These are the things that cause us to be content or not to be content. Our individual desires can make the difference between a person being truly happy with family or truly happy with fame, a person truly happy with being an entrepreneur or truly happy working for a corporation. The key is honesty. It's good to ask ourselves, have my desires thus far landed me on a truly satisfying course? Is the course I am on a reflection of my true desire? One must take caution here as well, because not every desire is worthy of fulfillment. The good thing is that with such an honest self-reflection, we can begin to make any changes necessary because change starts from within.

There are, however, boundaries to always keep in mind. These boundaries include considerations such as the legalities of the land in which we live, our religious beliefs, our health limitations. Again, the key is honesty. If we make this honest evaluation often enough, keeping in mind the relevant boundaries, our personal search for spectacular will begin to have rhythm and we will understand ourselves, we will feel good about who we are and about the choices we are faced with, and we will not be afraid to make decisions.

This is a book to help with that process. This is a book to motivate you to keep going. The chapters are short so as not to belabor the points. Anyone who knows me understands that I prefer to speak in simple terms, and I like to establish the point as quickly as possible. I happen to be a person of many ideas yet very few words.

This is a book to help talk things out, to help reason on matters, to help us not to lose our core selves, and quite frankly, to help us to hold ourselves accountable for the choices we do or don't make along our journey to spectacular. So, don't be afraid to make the changes. Change doesn't mean you don't have "it together". It's quite the opposite really. A healthy process for change often helps us to get to know ourselves and to be willing to make honest evaluations. Making necessary changes in our lives means we are willing to be a forward thinker, a progressive thinker, a critical thinker. Remember that our individual journey uniquely reflects our personal view of bright and shiny. This is just the beginning of our search for spectacular however long it may take.

Chapter 1

Why Me?

Why me? This happens to be one of the best and worst questions to ask. Depending that is on the emotional state and the motive behind the question. Depending on the motive, the results of asking this question can either be encouraging or discouraging and can have positive or negative effects on our life course. When we are reflecting on our life we want to do so reasonably. And we want to do so with a purpose of either being satisfied with the way things are going or being motivated for change. It's very important that we beware of self-pity.

"It ain't all roses" as the saying goes so chances are that when we make an evaluation of things in our life, we may not like what we see, where we are at, or how we got there. The choice though is ours right from the outset. We have a choice to decide why we are looking into things in the first place. What is the motive behind our evaluation?

The fact of the matter is that the specific reason for our self-analysis can come from one or many sources. It may have been triggered by an event, by something someone said, by something we saw or heard or felt, and so on and so forth.   Therefore, it's important to control the driving force behind our thought process. How can we be sure we are setting ourselves up to be motivated and encouraged instead of the opposite? We must recognize our end goal.

So many times, we start a process and are not successful because we don't know where we are going with it. Our work then seemingly has no purpose. What then do we do? We stop the process. We end the project. We throw away the data or the progress simply because it appears to be useless. We become discouraged that we have wasted our precious and very valuable time. This situation can be detrimental if applied to our lives.

We do not want to throw away the data of our lives because we are frustrated and don't know how to use what we have acquired from our analysis. This brings into play the importance of self-worth. Meaning, on a day-to-day basis we have to genuinely feel that we are worthy of happiness if we have achieved it, and worthy of change if we need it. We must use what we know about ourselves thus far. As we go through our lives and take our time of reflection, we first must briefly set in place our motive. We need to let ourselves know that this thought process is happening because we value ourselves and deserve to reassess things if need be. If we do see a need for change, or we come across an issue with a desire of past or present that needs to be adjusted, we must not wallow in it any further.

The motive, the end goal, is to take action if or when we realize that there are things we've been gravitating towards, the things we've deemed as bright and shiny, that have not led us to our spectacular. It's okay. Why? Here is where you ask, why me? Here is where you have control. Here is where you must be honest. Here is where you have the very data that reveals the why. Why are we experiencing the life we currently live? If we allow the data to work, it will also lead us to the how. How can we make changes that are definitive and purposeful in our journey to spectacular?

There certainly is power in asking why? The danger is to ask why me? And then decide that we have a particular set of circumstantial chance happenings that have made our lives less enjoyable than someone else's life. This type of summation is counterproductive to our improvement, to our journey.

We all know that we cannot and should not try to control every aspect of our lives. Time and unforeseen things happen every day that can cause our lives to take an undesirable turn. When something we consider to be a bad thing does happen in our lives, we still choose. We still do things and gravitate towards the choices desirable to us within our set of circumstances. Therefore, we must make definitive choices that are in harmony with our personal search for spectacular.   Perhaps when our circumstances changed our view of bright and shiny too made a shift. We then may find ourselves with new goals and on a new path full of new desires to meet those goals.

I personally have had some unexpected turns in my life. Each time, I have had to reevaluate what I like and what I need. I've had to realize that my new circumstances were not things I could change and while adjusting to them, my desires and my needs began to change as well. I've acquired a few more dynamics to my life, to my personality, what makes me physically comfortable, what type of people I want to be around, what I eat, the list goes on. Yes, my desires are still within the boundaries of my core values but some of them have changed none the less.   Sometimes, a new set of circumstances of which we cannot change, allows for a renewed uniqueness that can be embraced and harnessed.   It becomes part of our life journey and ultimately part of who we are.

The point is to be self-aware in order to remain progressive in our life journey. So, when the question arrives "Why me?" Let it be a source of motivation and encouragement helping us discover where we want to be, always in harmony with our moral and circumstantial boundaries, and always for the betterment of our lives. When change occurs, we want to take the opportunity to honestly evaluate what new things are bright and shiny to us now, directing and leading us in our search for spectacular.

Chapter 2

Eye Candy

None of us wants to consider ourselves shallow or superficial. But when we honestly consider the things that are desirable to us, how much depth do they have? It's a scientific fact that human beings have five major senses. These happen to be, in no sequential order, Sight, Touch, Taste, Hearing, and Smell. Some would even argue of a 6th that of an innate intuitive perception. The point is we do not want to limit our desires to what meets the physical eye when we have so much more, we can offer ourselves. How can we avoid this common worldly view? We can develop substance by becoming well learned. How, you ask? Read, Watch, Listen, Eat, and Explore the vast array of choices available to us.

There is a commonly used term "Don't knock it Till You Try It." This simply means, be open to trying new things and don't speak negatively of things of which you have no knowledge. Of course, we all know and have the right to decide that there are some things that we would just rather not be involved in investigating. We have the right to acknowledge that boundary. Let's remember though that our aim is to be sincere and honest in our choices and in our desires. We want to give ourselves the opportunity to have definitive reasons for what we do and don't do, what we desire and don't desire. The more options we have, the more choices we make (good or bad), the better we become acquainted with our true self. Again, we are not talking about going anywhere outside the boundaries of the law or our core values.

Why is this variety important? The more we know about our desires the more ownership we have of our choices. If we know we do or don't like something, someone, or someplace we won't hesitate to make a choice regarding that thing, that person, or that place. Not only does this provide us with a strong sense of self perception, but it helps us not to waste time in the decision-making process.

Some might argue that this is initially time consuming. But how long does it really take to try something new or even to learn about something new? Often times, the opportunity arises without any extra searching out on our part. We try it or learn about it and great, we love it, something added to our list of viable options. Or we try it or learn about it and too bad, we hate it, duly noted.

Additionally, we have been created with such reasoning ability to decide our feelings on an idea or item or type of person without actually having experienced it physically. We can use some of our other senses to help us determine choices. For example, I know that I have a predisposed liking to sunny and warm climates. Therefore, if given the option of living in Hawaii or Canada I, after investigating, reasoning on, and weighing the information carefully, would likely choose Hawaii. Now this of course is relative to only one detail, weather. Reasonably, there would be other things to consider. The more data compiled, the better prepared I'd be to make a choice. The point is, knowledge is power, in whatever form it comes. Let our decisions be based on fact, based on reason, and based on us as individuals. In relation to our search for spectacular, when we lead with information, we will be better equipped to make choices, know if we need to change our viewpoint, and further, decipher just how much adjustment we need to make.

What if we are confident that our decisions and desires have been coming from a reasoned upon and informed place and yet we still are not pleased with what we find when we evaluate of our lives? This may suggest that there is a need for adjustment. This conundrum speaks volumes to our reasoning ability or lack thereof. This may be a hard pill to swallow. However, I cannot stress enough the importance of honesty in this regard. Only a truly honest evaluation will allow us to clearly see any changes we may or may not need to make. I say "may not" because such an evaluation is not always doom and gloom. I know many people who are great decision makers. Some people are pleased with what their analysis beholds. They have made choices even years ago and continue to be happy with them, happy with their lives, and consistently so. Again, I say, they have found their rhythm and balance. They have found their moment of Spectacular.

Remember, it does not take much achievement for some to feel as if they have reached their moment where their desires and choices are married productively, whereas it takes much more success and achievement and time for others. This satisfaction of our analysis is relevant to our desires, which is relevant to our choices, which stems from our reasoning ability, which in turn comes from our knowledge. Oftentimes, there is more than what meets the eye. So do not limit yourself. Understand the power of knowledge in relation to your search for spectacular.

Chapter 3

The Power of Forethought

There is an ancient Proverb that reads a little something like this: "The naïve person believes every word, but the shrewd one thinks about each step." And yet another, like this: "The shrewd one sees the danger and protects himself, but the inexperienced keep right on going and suffer the consequences." Which one are you?

Inexperience is a part of life, yes. But the question is, how do we conquer our personal level of inexperience? Forethought is one of the most powerful tools for success. We may not be able to dream ourselves into an ideal situation but we sure can use a little imagination to prevent an undesirable outcome. How so? Think of a situation that you have experienced that left you wishing for a do over. What happened? Who was involved? And most importantly, what could have been avoided?

Hindsight is 20/20. That's what some people say when they realize the mistakes of times past. But I suggest, why not do a little thinking before the decision making? Why not try to "foresee the danger?" What we are not talking about here is being overly paranoid or overthinking every situation.   What I am encouraging is for us to offer ourselves just a brief moment, a pause, to simply think out our next step(s). Take time to slow down. Take time to consider. Take time to imagine the outcome of several scenarios.

Is this full proof? This process is absolutely not full proof! Not in the sense that you will always make the correct choice.   However, this process allows for accountability. The conflict is that some people do not want to be accountable for the outcome of their decisions so what do they often do? They choose not to think! They just jump right in.

Giving no forethought means that when things go awry it's not our fault. Right? Not exactly. Ignorance is not always bliss. Here is some food for thought. Although we cannot completely control every outcome in our lives, we can control our choices. We cannot be confident in our choices if we do not think things through. We will always wonder what we could have done. However, if we have already given forethought, even when we receive a less than desirable outcome, we will know what we could have done differently because we would have already considered other options in our choices, whether we made them or not. Perhaps we chose option A instead of option B and things didn't work out for the better. How is this helpful? We have gathered data. We have compiled a mental file of information that will be helpful for our future choices. When similar situations present themselves, we are now better equipped to recognize them for what they are, to weigh our options, and to make better choices.

If we do not give forethought and instead simply react, we are not allowing our brains to identify and compartmentalize information. Scientifically speaking our brain is not a muscle but it can be treated as one. When we use our thinking ability, we provide exercise for our minds. This type of mental stimulation allows our thinking faculties to become stronger and faster. The more thought we provide, the easier this process becomes because our mental filing system becomes more organized. Our options become clearer, and our choices become more defined. We become shrewd, the type of person in charge of our desires and choices and lives because we are knowledgeable and experienced. "Make wise choices" as my oldest son use to say when he was in kindergarten. It's amazing how we can forget such a simple concept as adults.

This leads me to another thought. There is an underestimated amount of power in using and accepting the word no. Try it. Say it out loud. "No." If you want to have successful outcomes, know about no. The word no is what I like to call a guidance word. From the moment it is spoken or heard it creates boundaries. We can use these boundaries to help us with forethought.

When thinking on a situation, we may hit a touchy scenario. We, then must decide if we are willing to move forward with a particular option, based on the results that it may bring. Of course, this involves considering all of our options and deciding the good and the bad of each option. What is interesting about this process is that not always will there be an option that appears to be "good". Sometimes all of our options seem to be ones that will produce positive results. However, sometimes there are only options that appear to be unfavorable.

Since there is oftentimes a combination of possible outcomes, we must be able to decipher what some call the lesser or greater of two evils. If all options do not seem as though they will reap favorable results but we still, however, must make a choice, this is where it is important to know the no that we are willing to endure. Know which outcomes we are okay with experiencing. Again, understand that we don't have full control, but to be able to think on these things gives us a type of power over our lives that promotes solid decision-making practices, helping us to recognize our honest feelings and desires, helping us to identify our strengths and weaknesses, and ultimately assists us in our search for spectacular, and create a life journey that we can proudly take ownership of.

Chapter 4

They Don't Get It

In literature and drama, there is a term everyman. This term basically means someone who is ordinary and yet has experienced extraordinary circumstances and therefore the audience, you and I, are able to easily identify with. Wouldn't it be nice if we were everyone's everyman? Wouldn't it be nice if no matter what feeling we feel, what desire we have, what path we choose, what journey we are on and no matter what events take place, and no matter what decisions we made, everyone just gets it. They don't judge, they don't gossip, they don't feel any negativity. They let us be because they understand. Does this sound too good to be true? It does because it is.

Although we may have some people in our corner that cut us some slack when we make choices, the fact is that many people just don't agree with the choices that we make. Even those closest to us, those who do cut us some slack, don't always necessarily identify with our process.

Most of the time, they accept our choices because they appreciate us and respect us enough not to give us a hard time. We must accept the fact that people are not always going to understand or appreciate our life journey, the desires that guide our choices, or the decisions that we make along the way. If we can't accept this fact, we cannot be true to ourselves. If we feel as though we need the approval of others, if we find ourselves constantly seeking the advice of others, we should ask ourselves, whose journey am I on?

True, there are benefits with seeking another person's perspective on a matter. The caution here is to be sure to seek another perspective from individuals that are able to be empathetic to our personal circumstances. If a person cannot visualize our specific circumstances, what we are going thru, how we may feel, what problems we may face, and therefore be able to present advice from that vantage point, from our perspective, then their advice may not be practical for us.   This is important because we want to make sure we are making decisions relevant to our core selves.

It is only normal for us to want to share and express the topsy-turvies of our lives with the people whom we care about. The responsibility though lies with us. We must have our internal radar online, up and running and able to identify the person or persons in our lives that are beneficial to us in this regard. It is also, up to us to accept the fact that quite honestly, some people just don't get it. Most people just don't get it. And that is perfectly okay.

All too often we react to another person's opinion in a way that is not proactive to our process. We adopt their opinion as our own. This can be harmful because we then lose ownership of our choices. We then become misguided in our feelings and desires. This then leads us to being frustrated and puts us in a position where we become unidentifiable to ourselves. This is the breeding ground for feelings of insecurity, uncertainty, and vulnerability. Or even worse, we may lose ourselves altogether and before we know it, we are going down the path of someone else's journey.

Do not misunderstand my words, I know there are times when we take the high road and decide to simply understand and accept another person's opinion to perhaps avoid a negative situation. In fact, that's sometimes best, simply agree to disagree. What we want to avoid, however, is creating an ulterior persona that is easily persuaded to accept the desires and choices that are not true to who we are, what we want, and where we want to be. Remember it is important to remain our unique selves. We do not want to lose what makes us, us.

Instead of existing with the hope that others will understand and accept the choices we make. Appreciate those who have the knack for empathy and can provide us with an opinion valuable to our personal journey. As for everyone else, be okay if they just don't get it.

Chapter 5

Don't Forget

I'm a firm believer that the things a person experiences in life help them in the process of developing wisdom. Some people call this being worldly-wise. True, experience is only one source of wisdom. There are other sources. Education, Communication, and Experience I'd have to say are at the top of my list. There is something that must be said about experience though that just makes stuff stick. Well let's just say it sticks for many people. I am aware that there exist a people who, no matter what they experience, just don't seem to be able to find the lesson. However, when we are able to learn from experiences, the happenings of the past, whether good or bad become legendary in our personal history book.

The knowledge we gain from our experiences is what we begin to use to make choices and decisions that can be considered as wise. These stories can be the building blocks that help us to develop in a way that is truly authentic to us.   True, some people sometimes experience the same or similar things. But no one truly experiences things the way you do because they have not experienced them as you, through your eyes. How can we be sure to take advantage of the things that happen in our lives? We must be present each and every minute.

I must admit, I have the worst memory. I could have just said something, saw something, heard something and moments later, I have the hardest time with recollection. I'm saddened by this really. Especially since there have been unforeseen circumstances in my life that have negatively impacted this aspect of my day to day. For me to recall events at a later date, I often have to make a conscious effort to truly focus on what is happening at the present.

I'm not referring to having some sort of out of body, subconscious, meditative experience as some may think. I'm just saying it helps to focus. Look around, smell, and listen. Use your senses to create presence. This helps to give your mind and body more substance to remember each experience by.   It creates more detail to each happening so that it is easier to call moments back to mind.

I truly understand that not every experience is a desirable one to recall. We all have had and will continue to have bad experiences. I feel though, that even the bad experiences can be learned from and therefore should be remembered. Oftentimes we find ourselves again in a situation that we had already negatively experienced prior. How does this keep happening to us? Why are we here again? What do I keep doing wrong? We may ask. The short answer just may be that we forgot. We have forgotten the bad choices that led us into this less than desirable situation. We must not forget!

Ask ourselves, what is worse, remembering a bad situation or event that we experienced and recalling the hurt or pain that came from it, or would it be worse to completely forget about a bad situation, suppressing the hurt and pain, thinking that we've gotten past it only to relive it all again and again because we didn't remember how to avoid it? Surely, we want to keep the lesson. We want to remember the details in order to gain the knowledge from the experience so that we can truly overcome it and avoid repeating the same mistakes. The same is to be said about the positive experiences we have had in the past. We want to repeat positive experiences as much as we can. Don't we?

The more we remember, the better able we are to identify similar happenings and realize what type of outcome is more likely to be had. By being present in each situation we are able to be more proactive in our lives. This motivates us to take responsibility in our choices, knowing, based on what we remember, if we are on a course of action that will reap positive results. We begin to understand the choices we are making. We understand the things that are desirable to us, and we can recognize if the desire is healthy for us and will lead to a positive end result or just the opposite. If we don't forget the negative, we can take decisive action to make different choices. If we don't forget the positive, we can be confident in our choices, in our life course, in our search for spectacular. Whether the outcome was good or bad, the point is don't forget.

Chapter 6

Get Out of the Harbor

Have you ever had one of those dreams where someone is chasing you or you are running for some other reason, and you seem to be getting nowhere? Or a dream where something terrible is happening and you try to scream but nothing comes out? Life without forgiveness can be just like that, stagnant.

Think of a harbor full of ships large and small. Holding on to resentment is like being stuck in the harbor. Everyone else is sailing along. We are weighed down. Our anchor won't lift.

When it comes to our search for spectacular, holding on to resentment is counterproductive. True, it's challenging to move on when we feel hurt by others. We should ask ourselves though, has the other party moved on? Oftentimes we find ourselves stuck, constantly replaying an event that we have experienced, something someone has done or said to us that left us feeling slighted or pained. If we can take a second to refocus, we may be able to clearly see an important point. The other party has "left the building" as people often put it. They have moved on into further aspects of their lives some maybe not even knowing that they have hurt us at all.

This does not mean that we do not have the right to inform these ones of how they have made us feel. We absolutely have that right. We don't have to pretend the offense has not taken place or minimize how it has made us feel. Perhaps we do inform them, and things are cleared up and we all feel so much better in the end. But what happens if we express our hurt and yet, we do not get a favorable response in return? What do we do then? Sadly, the tendency is to build hate, resentment and disdain towards the person or persons who have hurt us. But what does this do for us? What does this do to us?

The truth is resentment really only hurts us. Holding on to these types of feelings is similar to expecting someone else to feel hurt when we stub our toe, or get a paper cut, or hurt ourselves in any other type of way. No other person feels our pain in the same way we do. Unfortunately, all too often, not even the afflicter.

Initially we may have been dealt with treacherously by someone and thus encounter the feelings that come along with such dealings, however, harboring continuous negative feelings is a choice. To hold onto continuous negative feelings is our choice. We can't make that choice and expect others to feel our pain. That type of pain is ours to feel, no one else.

To let go and move on is our choice as well. Forgiveness is a choice. Something that can help is to put the shoe on the other foot. Yep, we all know we have been the offender in the past. We have said and done things that we can only hope we can be forgiven for. I hate to sound cliché but what if we take a note from the Golden Rule and treat other people in a way that we would desire to be treated. Don't we want to be forgiven? There is a saying that goes something like "Let Go and Let God Deal with It." Maybe that doesn't do anything for you, but neither does resentment.

Resentment can only build negativity which can be harmful to our heart, mind, and soul. So, as we make decisions on our path of life. As we accept the things we desire. As we reject the things we don't want. Never forget that forgiveness gives us power. It gives us power over ourselves. We cannot control the actions of other people. However, the more we forgive, the more we gain the recognition for ourselves that we are in control. We control our emotions, we control our actions, and we control our choices. Get out of the harbor. We have the power to uplift ourselves and sail on. Let go of resentment and forgive.

Chapter 7

Stand Tall

Why is it that so many people seem to give themselves so much leeway and excuses for the choices they make but they can see so clearly why everyone else's decisions are wrong? "There are no judgment's here." This is something that someone says when other people are telling them about some way that they feel or something that they have done. It is meant to put people at ease. Why? What is the reason for saying this? There is most often going to be a judgement of some sort.

People judge other people. People know they are being judged. It happens often. Especially when it comes to the mistakes we make. I for one do not think it is my place to judge a person as being good or bad. I do however agree with making an evaluation of a person's actions. I'd have to say that Judgments and Evaluations are close cousins. A judgment is more concrete. An evaluation often allows for more reasoning. Judgments are based on hard laws. Evaluations are based on principles.

When a person allows themselves to evaluate the actions or mistakes of another person, they are allowing room to examine the scenario under many different circumstances, values, and principles. Why is this process useful?

By evaluating in this way, a person can reason on why or why not to take a particular course of action themselves. In this way an individual is able to judge for themselves what choice they would make based on productive evaluations, instead of simply judging other people as good or bad for the choices they've made. It's easy for someone to say that they will not do something because it is wrong or that they will do something because it is the right thing to do. Most likely, though, when we are actually in the situation, things are not always so black and white.

When we adjust, and evaluate the scenario inserting our own circumstances, values, and principles, we get a better and clearer picture of what actions we really would be willing to take. We begin to see our own strengths and our own weaknesses. We begin to judge and evaluate ourselves which is much more productive. Our personal values become more visible. This type of assessment helps us to stand tall and stand firm in our own decision-making process including making needed adjustments. We train ourselves to think deeply on and evaluate the actions of others not to pass judgement on them but to better our selves and grow as individuals. Who knows, we may find that there is good that can be learned in what others have done.

When we realize that we don't just make choices on a whim. When we realize that we have learned how to evaluate our decisions and those of others productively, then we gain freedom. We gain the freedom to remain steady in our choices because we become more and more skilled in weighing multiple options. We also gain the freedom to change our course just the same if once weighed, once evaluated, we realize that our current course isn't working for us or isn't productive. Remember, everyone else has made their choices so don't be ashamed of yours.

Even if our course has changed before, we don't have to feel as if we can't make another shift. We don't want to let other people hold us to a path that we realize is not right for us. When we learn to evaluate our choices, our likes, our dislikes, and our lives, we are not scared to be accountable for our decisions. We know we have contemplated what we truly feel is the best course of action. And we therefore are not afraid to take action or take the next steps in whatever situation we are in, even if that step is backwards.

I used to think that just because I was deep in certain situations that it was too late to back out. I used to think that going backwards made me less brave. People mistake going backwards with not progressing.

Sometimes we have to go backwards in order to move forward. This may sound a bit cliché but think of athletes in track and field. We usually give most of the accolades to the runners but there are other events. The long jumpers for example, if you've ever watched them then you may have noticed that they don't just halfheartedly take a leap. They take a mental calculation and may even step forward, then backward, forward, then backward, until they feel they are ready to take off, springing forward and outward as far as they can. Think too of a disc thrower, how many times do they circle around before they release? Do these players work any less than the sprinters and distance runners? They just work a little different to get the results that they are seeking.

The point is this, don't be afraid to back up or even turn around. Don't be ashamed of your process. Sometimes you don't realize you are in a negative situation until you are "knee deep in it" as the saying goes. While it is often best to give the forethought mentioned in Chapter 3, it isn't always practical, or we may just forget that step. The situation we are experiencing could have taken such twists and turns that the outcome becomes unrecognizable, completely unpredictable. What then?

It doesn't matter at what point we realize that a situation is not good for us. Once the evaluation is made and it becomes clear, this is the point we have power. We don't always feel powerful because we may be discouraged, but there is always a way out. Find it and take it. Never feel that you don't have a choice. Make a choice and stand tall.

It's better to recognize our mistakes. It's also good to evaluate the mistakes of others, in order to learn what decisions we are willing to make under certain circumstances. This does not mean that we judge others around us as being either good or bad persons. However, what this does mean is that we are willing to evaluate what actions others have taken and weigh them against what actions we will take and why. Consciously and thoughtfully make the choice that is right for you. Give yourself the power to stand tall.

Chapter 8

Change of Life

For some it's called the change of life. For many it's referred to as a midlife crisis. Yet, still for others it's called the bloom of youth. What it's called simply depends on the stage we are at within this thing called life. There are stages that we come upon where who we think we are, or what we think we like, or where we think we want to go suddenly becomes fuzzy at best. We take a look at ourselves, and we just don't have a clue. Too many people become frantic, they panic and full speed ahead they go. The problem is they don't know where they are going because they no longer can identify with who they are, what they like, want, or need.

Have you ever gotten lost? I mean physically lost, maybe as a young child or even as an adult for that matter. I have more than once. One of the times that I can recall as a child was when I was on a trip out of state with one of my closest friends and her family. One of our recreational events was going to an arcade. While we were there, I got lost. I don't know what happened, at one point we were all together. The next thing I knew, I was all alone. Well, there were other people around me of course but no one recognizable. I don't quite remember all of the details (remember I have a terrible memory; I wish I was more present in that moment) but what I do remember is panic. I felt an almost overwhelming feeling of panic because my surroundings that I was once comfortable with became instantly, shockingly confusing.

This is how our lives can become in an instant. One moment things feel comfortable, and secure. The next moment we become unsure, and we begin to panic. Don't panic. Chances are, these are fleeting moments that we can attribute to nothing more than a temporary change in our minds and/or bodies. What do I mean? From a scientific standpoint some of the primary functions of our bodies rely heavily on our hormones. The problem presents itself when we produce more or less hormones than usual, or even when we produce different, imbalanced levels of one or more hormones than another. Too many stories have I heard where this has been the case for someone and instead of waiting for the balance or better yet finding the tools to help find the balance, poor choices are made with lasting or worse, devastating consequences.

When we find ourselves at a similar time in our lives where there is nothing recognizable that makes us feel as if we are home and happy, where nothing looks bright or shiny, we may need to just wait it out. I can attest to the fact that sometimes work needs to be done and practical tools need to be found and used to help us regain our internal balance. This doesn't mean that in the meantime we can't do anything to bring us joy and comfort, but we may want to be careful of doing things that are drastic. Why? Sometimes drastic changes can feel exhilarating and leave us feeling empowered, especially when we feel lost. But if we aren't careful, we may be left feeling only regret in the end. Sometimes our bodies are just off balanced, and we need to "level out". This takes time. This takes patience. This sometimes takes effort. How do we know when we really need a change and when we just think we need a change?

Honest evaluation is the key. I've said this before. When we are honest with ourselves, we can avoid a tremendous amount of heartache. Typically, we know ourselves and we can decipher if we are just nitpicking as they say. If we realize that lately we have a problem, an issue with something or someone around us that never really concerned us prior, and we can't really give a definite answer as to why, then chances are that the issue is within ourselves. We may have to do a little soul searching and find out how we can maintain happiness in our current situation.

Now, as you know I am all about change, I encourage it but what I cannot cosign and encourage is change in spite of truth. We must be honest about our motives. We also must be realistic about our current circumstances in life. Meaning, we must count all cost. We must weigh all options and measure all sides of a scenario. We must determine the motive behind our feelings. Here again is where we hold power.

There is no absolute gauge that measures whether our feelings or level of selfishness is harmful or is warranted. We are the only ones who really know the honest truth. In order to know the honest truth though, we have to make sure we are being honest in our thinking. Have you ever had the tendency during these times to manipulate matters to mirror how we feel? I know I've done this. If we feel someone annoys us, we may try to amplify their mistakes or flaws to make it appear that they are the problem when in all honesty we may be the ones who need to make the adjustment, or our own feelings may be off balance. No one wants to realize that they are in the wrong. But wouldn't it be best to make this determination prior to making a drastic decision that we will sooner or later regret. We must be able to check ourselves and make personal corrections.

It's possible for us to be on a great path, one that has been bringing us happiness and success. Then, suddenly we go through one of these changes of life or something similar and nothing is how we want it. We don't want to lose our footing. So, during times like these it's best to tread carefully until we feel once again confident about the path we are on and whether we actually even need change. We may find that things are alright just the way they are, and we may be forevermore grateful that we didn't take any extraordinary measures regarding change.

Everyone goes through some sort of life adjusting process. Just be sure that the choices we make are choices that help us progress, decisions that are in harmony with our core values, and traits that are true to our uniqueness, not decisions that will leave us with regret and ultimately put us light years away from spectacular.

Chapter 9

Take Hold

Let's recap. What is a search for spectacular? I had a friend once tell me that she doesn't look for something spectacular to happen in her life. She said that she doesn't make her choices based on something bigger or better. That's not necessarily what I'm referring to when I speak about spectacular.

As I explained to my friend, we all are guided in our lives by our preferences, the things we gravitate towards, the things we view as bright and shiny. Everyone's choices are different because everyone's desires are different. We all have a way that we are living our lives. Our paths are authentic to us.

True, we all have influences that we accept as our own along the way. Once again, we only accept these things because they are desirous to us. We build on these influences as we develop into who we are. These influences affect our choices. Our choices affect our path.

Our path affects our moment or moments. There is no hard fast rule of what a successful moment is any more than there being a definite successful path. Our uniqueness determines our views on this.

To search, simply put, is to seek carefully or thoroughly. It's a verb. This means taking action. It involves playing an active role in our life. It involves being aware. This requires forward thinking, progressive thinking, and critical thinking.

By living our lives in a way that we make definite choices based on what we value, and by thoroughly and carefully considering our options and our abilities, we will have more moments that stand out and catch our eye. We will have more moments that we truly can appreciate. We are more likely to have moments that are spectacular to us. As those times occur, take hold of each moment, embrace them, and shine bright. Naturally, as your light shines, others with be attracted, but these moments are yours, no one else's.

The majority of us want lives that we can feel good about. We want to feel confident in the lives that we live. Most of us want lives that provide pleasant memories. Most of us are in search of our moment when we begin to see the positive results, rhythm, and productive connection between our desires, which are the things, and persons we view as bright and shiny, and the choices that we make because of gravitating towards them. That balance is something that makes our lives appear beautiful in a dramatic and eye-catching way. Most of us are seeking this type of life. Most of us are searching for spectacular.

Chapter 10

Done Searching? Give Yourself Permission

There is something to be said about where we find ourselves when we take an honest look. One of the hardest realities for me to accept was that I am right where I've given myself permission to be.

I used to wonder (even sometimes scoff) at the persons that don't have the credentials yet offer the "help", the persons without the experience, yet rocking all of the "titles" i.e. Coach, Leader, Expert, Mentor, etc. Then I realized an important fact. They have allowed themselves to serve. Whether they are truly qualified or not is beside the point. They feel as though they are worthy, qualified, and able to offer value. They have given themselves permission to Lead, to Coach, to Thrive.

If you are anything like me, you are good at the learning part of life. I excel as a student. I've always given myself permission to sit in that seat. Let me ask though, as a student in the School of Life, what would happen if we gave ourselves permission to draw on the knowledge we have gained through our experiences and assign them the value that allows us to teach about them with confidence, lead with enthusiasm, and to truly thrive in that space?

Here's the hard truth, a primary difference between the Leaders and the Followers is that Leaders give themselves permission to lead. What we don't want to do is make the mistake of being a chronic student, searching for any and every title behind our name.

Although education and qualifications are important, the credibility is not always in the credentials. People look for the light. People believe if we appear to believe. If we never give ourselves permission to be a success, if we never give ourselves permission to be spectacular, then we will never shine bright enough to attract.

The good and bad of it all is that we are the ones in control of how much permission to give ourselves. We never know how much value we hold until we offer it to others. Do not be a treasure hoarder. If we ever find ourselves stuck in a space where we aren't necessarily searching, or we don't feel that a change in course is what we need, and yet we are just not feeling productive, we may not be living up to our full potential, we may just need to give ourselves permission to shine right where we are, share our story, and teach, and lead, and be the bright and shiny for someone else's search for spectacular.

References & Key Terms

Spectacular-Beautiful in a dramatic and eye-catching way.(https://www.google.com/search?q=spectacular+definition&ie+UTF-8&oe=UTF-8&hl=em-us&client=safari)

Moment of Spectacular- Our moment when we begin to see the positive results, rhythm, and productive connection between our desires, which are the things or people we view as bright and shiny, and the choices that we make because of gravitating towards them.

The Spectacular balance is something that makes our lives appear "beautiful in a dramatic and eye-catching way". Naturally, our course then attracts others and becomes the "bright and shiny" for someone else that is Searching for Spectacular.

About The Author

Ryan is a wife, mom, and a woman of faith. Over the years she has been successful in acquiring skills, licensures, or certifications for various fields such as Massage, Cosmetology, Real Estate, Nutrition, and Aromatherapy. She is passionate about being able to care for her family and continuing to better herself by supporting others, building lasting relationships, and developing a mindset that withstands unforeseen change. It is her understanding of how positivity and encouragement effects our overall well-being that drives her to be a bright light of motivation for people around her.

In 2018, after experiencing an array of physical ailments, and surgeries that ultimately lead to extreme fatigue, hormone imbalances, and more, a few years prior, Ryan was forced to leave a career in the Salon and Spa Industry that she loved dearly. Shortly thereafter, Ryan began to seek wellness options for the mind and body.

In 2020 after another job loss due to the Covid-19 Pandemic, Ryan launched her company Ryan Ashley's Essentials. Through Ryan Ashley's Essentials she has been able to direct people to tools such as essential oils, wellness items, and other creations that are designed to motivate, encourage, and help people develop an upbuilding mindset that keeps them energized and focused on accomplishing their goals. Searching for Spectacular fits right in line with her established portfolio and is a testament to her desire to continue to offer as much value to her audience as she can.

Social Media & Business Links (2022)

Instagram:
https://www.instagram.com/ryanashley4real/

Facebook Page: Wellness & Smiles w/ Ryan Ashley

Young Living Brand Partner Sponsor/Enroller ID #14584924
Natural Living Store:
https://www.youngliving.com/us/en/referral/14584924

Website:
Allthingsryanashley.com

"Here is where your light starts shining brighter than ever before."

-Ryan Ashley W.